T0128556

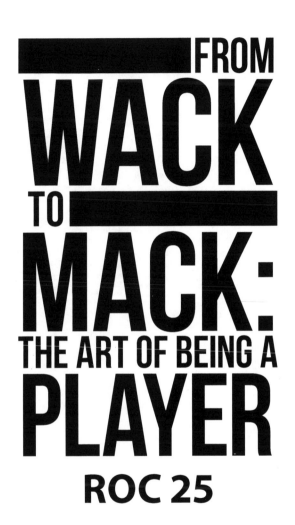

FROM WACK TO MACK: THE ART OF BEING A PLAYER

ROC 25

authorHOUSE®

AuthorHouse™
1663 Liberty Drive
Bloomington, IN 47403
www.authorhouse.com
Phone: 1 (800) 839-8640

Published by AuthorHouse 01/20/2020

ISBN: 978-1-7283-4402-7 (sc)
ISBN: 978-1-7283-4401-0 (e)

Library of Congress Control Number: 2020901158

CONTENTS

INTRO

This isn't for the guy who wants to win the girl in apartment 2B, or the one who wants to date the cute girl in his Western Civ class, or the girl that sits alone in the coffee shop. This book is intended for the guy who wants to fuck all three girls. Sure, if you want to use this book as a means of "winning the heart" of such said girl, cool. I won't tell anyone you used a book designed to get multiple women at your disposal.

The ones who are tired of not having stories to tell. The ones who are tired of getting rejected and want to be 'The Man". The Player is a chameleon. Comfortable in any surrounding. Can be in a room full of Eighteen-year-old girls and then in

a room full of Fifty-year-old women and still feel comfortable at least half the room would sleep with him. A Player is like a Mob Boss, everyone knows he committed the crime, but it can never be proven. You are always going to be indicted, you should never be convicted.

Some of you on these dating sites/apps send pics of your dick to a girl, before you even say hi. Are y'all for real? No Dime is going talk to you doing that. That porn you watch warped your brain. Those are paid actresses. If you don't have the cash, you ain't getting a Porn Star (talking from experience). Anyway, the problem with a lot of you guys is that you don't know how to talk to girls, either because you are scared or you simply don't know. Before you know how to talk to girls, you must look right first. If you look like a scrub, no girl is going to hear what you have to say. So Player, let's get to it and go from wack to mack!

GROOMING

A ppearances are everything. I don't care what anyone says, it's true. The goal is to have a look that will be able to attract anyone. Edge your beard and hairlines for a sharp crisp look. It shows that you care about you care about detail and possibly your place and car probably look nice as well. If you're the guy that liked to have the real long beard (ZZ Top like) you are going to get attention but limit the girls, you will attract. If you are going to have a beard, edge it and keep the lines sharp. It shouldn't be more than ¼ of an inch off your face (think about how her face feels if she's kissing you) Even if you have big hair like an afro, edge the front and the back isn't sharp, keep that nice as well. If you

are one of those with bushy eyebrows or unibrow dudes, if you think it's holding you back, take care of it. Things that you are insecure about you can either do two things, embrace it or do something about it. Some of you guys have a lot of body hair. I never had that issue, but if you like it, go for it. I like looking strong and muscular and all that hair can cover up all your hard work especially if you exercise. As for shaving, the minimum blades I use it at least two no particular brand, the same with shaving cream. Speaking of that, the leads to another popular discussion if 'manscaping'.

Personally, I can't stand pubic hair. If you are one of those with a jungle bush, trim it at least. I shave it all off and the ladies love it. I've never heard one woman complain about me not having any hair down there. Plus, it'll make it easier to convince her to shave it off if she is hairy down there as well. Some of you guys got crazy pimples and my only advice, is I used Clearisil, but talk to a doctor to see what the right medication would be. For teeth, I have crooked bottom teeth and I still do the damn thing. I never got braces or

anything like that and most likely won't. I also have a gap in my front tooth as well. Confidence in myself (remember when I said, things you are insecure about you can embrace or do something about it) helps overcompensate that deficiency. I do admit, I never thought it was a problem and it ever held me back, but I do floss my teeth, with a brand called 'Plackers'. I know dentists say use the wax one because you can get deeper below the gumline but the Plackers come in a resealable bag, they have a pick on it too, Use it and throw it away. Simple. I use Crest Complete whitening toothpaste and I swear by Listerine Total Care, the purple bottle. That is amazing. Twice a day, and you are good to go. As it comes to body wash, I'm always trying new body washes. You know how it goes, once you like one, they stop making it (bring back Axe Touch). Deodorant though, I do swear by Old Spice, Sweat Defense Pure Sport Plus. I rub until it's clear and for me, I don't get stains on my clothes when I use it and it's a fresh scent. Cologne, you can't go wrong with Curve by Liz Clairborne, but you re broke, any Body Spray will do. I can't

stress this enough, keep your nails and ears clean. Especially before meeting up with a girl, you don't want earwax falling out or for her to see have longer fingernails than her and you haven't cleaned underneath them at least. Cut your toenails too, because you never know what could happen on the first date.

CLOTHING

lright, Player, we got grooming down, so I got you prettified and sexified. I'm not saying everything must be name brand, don't worry. You should have at least, a nice designer belt and shoes in your arsenal. They all can't be Brick and Mortar Specials. Yes, you have at least one Polo. I mean Ralph Lauren Polo, not golf shirt (unless you are playing golf that day maybe). The days of baggy jeans are gone. This isn't 2001 Plus you have to show them sneakers off too. So, let's keep it simple. You should have at least three pair of Khakis, Blue, Beige and Black. Your shirts should all be able to go with that. I don't like ties, but you should have at least one universal tie that can go with any dress

shirt and pant combo. Go all black with a blazer, tie, socks, shoes and pants. Too easy not to mess up even if you don't know colors. Any dress shirt will work. When you are in a dress outfit, wear black or gray socks. If not, you'll look like a clown who doesn't know better and now you know better if you didn't before. Jeans is always touchy depending on the type of person you are, you a baller, skater or whatever. You must represent who you are. I got it. I represent Players. I don't wear baggy jeans because that attracts only a certain type of girl. I'm looking to attract all the girls. So, I wear jeans that fit nicely around my waist. I do wear a belt sometimes. I have two belts, one with a big designer belt buckle, and a business belt that's also a designer one that's more subtle but you know what it is. I'm not a watch guy or jewelry so I'm not going to tell you to get the Mr. T starter kit. I like digital watches, it's possible to get a real nice one that isn't tactical looking if you don't like one with hands. You should have a stylish one. Have the appearance of sensibility at least, Player. I get it, some of you guys aren't sneakerheads and think "Oh, that shouldn't

matter". If you ever had a girl comment on your shoes, it's intoxicating I don't care what anyone says. I've bought clothes just to match the sneakers Show that you are into sine trends and you are into some trends. I'm not saying you have to rock Nikes, Adidas or anything like that but it's not a bad idea. I admit, I go to Outlets and TJ Maxx, ain't no shame in my game. Gotta do what I gotta do. The moral of the story, wear that clothes that fit your shape, stay color coordinated, look stylish, have a couple of brand names and you can't go wrong.

YOUR PLACE

I f the people you live with are slobs, keep at least your room and the bathroom clean. Shower Mats get disgusting, so get an area carpet. It dries quickly and never gets nasty. You should have towels, washcloth, body wash, shampoo and conditioner for designated for a girl. Believe me, only thoughts that will go through her head, she'll be either impressed and or think you are a Player but who cares if you get her to sleep with you. For those with roommates, just have a designated spot in your room for all that if you can't put all that in your bathroom. If you have a flat screen less than 32 inches, (how she is going see what's on TV with a small screen) you need to upgrade, man. Garbage should be taken out, dishes should be

done, your place should be immaculate. I clean my place once a week so when I have a girl over, I don't have a lot to clean when I do have someone coming over and just concentrate on getting ready. If you don't have at least two pillows, invest the five dollars and handle your business, Also, get a pillow cover as well that matches your bed spread too. Even the bed should be color coordinated or have a theme. If you still got the Pokémon blanket or anything that is kiddish …give it to your sibling or to someone else and get on your grown man shit. This is going to sound crazy, have the condoms by the bed, you don't want to walk away from the bed, turn the light on or risk her not being in the mood because it's taking you forever to get or looking for them. I stay with Trojan Spermicidal Lubricant. Haven't gotten anyone pregnant using them (knock on wood). Make sure your cellphone is on silent, not vibrate and lock screen on. Whoever gets at you, you can find out later, promise.

BODY

Recap, we got grooming, clothing and your place on point. There are levels to this. What if your body looks a mess? Listen, if you are ok, with your body whether you twenty or more pounds overweight, or you are a hard gainer, then skip this chapter. You and I both know, that girls prefer a dude with big arms, toned body and six pack for abs. It's just a reality and if you want the Hotties or any girl for the most part that's the look that's going attract them. The guy with the nice abs beats the guy with the pot belly feel me. Now, for those who have a gym membership and aren't getting results then I have simple solution. Get Ronnie Coleman's book "Hardcore". Changed my life. He won Mr. Olympia

eight years in a row, the premier bodybuilding competition, which tied the record with Lee Haney and one more than Arnold Schwarzenegger. He gives his whole workout routine with detailed pics and a sample diet plan. Even if you don't want to look that muscular, it's a good base of the type of exercises to change your physique. He doesn't really give his ab routine. Don't worry, I will give mine. If you don't have a gym membership, here is my home workout too. You are going to need some equipment, a pull up bar that you can put up on the door, yoga ball, dumbbells or resistance bands with a handle, ab wheel, and a sit up bar. If you can't afford any equipment, I got you too but for those who can, I do three sets of pull ups and super set with biceps curls, this why you need either resistance bands or dumbbells. I usually do fifteen reps for biceps curls. A superset is when you do one exercise and another back to back, So I'll do one set of pull ups and no rest go to bicep curls. I'll do that two more times then go to abs. If you can't do pull ups yet, do two sets of push-ups or dips on a chair. First for those who can, you want to

get ab straps, the one that Valeo make I love because it has a metal D ring. Put tape where you put the D ring, so you don't potentially scratch the bar too bad. So, you put your arm through the straps, you want to work your way up to fifteen reps per exercise. So you want to do fifteen reps or ab raises with your legs straight, bent, bicycle kick, (it's performed how it sounds, each leg is one rep, so when you lift your left leg and right leg, that's one rep, lift your left leg and right leg again, that's two reps and so one) and side to side for obliques. This is tricky. You start knees one side and you must lift your legs over to the other side, then lift your legs to the other side and that's one rep. Don't swing your legs from side to side. You do that you aren't doing shit. remember to lift your pelvis and not just lift your legs when you are doing the straight leg and bent legs, to get more ab development. When you do all four of those exercises once (ten second break in between the exercises for an example, fifteen straight leg ab raises, ten second rest then fifteen straight bent leg ab raises and so on) then repeat two more times. After that, you want to do one

hundred sit ups, this is where the sit up bar comes in. Doesn't matter how many sets you do, if you get one hundred reps in. If you can't afford a sit up bar it's usually about fifteen dollars, but you can put your feet underneath the couch or just on the ground and knock them out. For the next day you are going to start off with two sets of push-ups close arm and the two sets of wide arm. After that then two sets of dips. For abs, this is where you need the Ab Wheel, Yoga Ball and a sit up bar. You want to do fifty reps on the ab wheel. It's like how you've seen people do it. Get on your knees, both hands on the ab wheel handle and roll out. Once you bring the ab wheel back to your legs, that's one rep. After that, get on the Yoga ball, put your heels on the ball with your back on the ground. Bring the ball in, knees to your chest. As you progress to make it more challenging, lift your lower back off the ground when you bring your knees in. That's one rep right there. Next you want to get in the plank on the Yoga ball on the ball and bring your knees close to your arms for fifty reps. Then get in the ab straps for obliques and do the same

exercise you did yesterday. After you do all that, you want to do some cardio. Me personally, I go jogging for the minimum for thirty min straight for at least four times a week, six days a week the most. If you can't jog or you haven't done any cardio for years, start with walking for thirty min and eventually jog for a little bit then time yourself to see how long you can jog for before you get out of breath. If its ten seconds, (hopefully you aren't that bad but if you are so be it) then after that walk for a min then jog again for ten seconds. Do this until you can run for thirty minutes straight. I know there are a lot of you who hate running, go on YouTube or whatever and there are whole bunch of alternatives for aerobics or HIIT (High Intensity Interval Training). Find what you like and get it in. Repeat those exercises and do cardio at least three more times throughout the week. One piece of equipment I love is called Bowflex Uppercut. I was able to get in crazy shape with it. I was doing about one thousand pushups a week on it, but you can do other upper body exercises as well. Also was doing six hundred reps for abs on it as well. It's about one

hundred dollars but it's worth every penny. It comes with a wall chart for exercises but If you can do those three times a week and exercise for a total six times a week total that would be amazing. Don't be lazy and make time. It's about not just looking good with clothes on. She should be imagining what you look like with clothes off and you meeting perhaps surpassing her expectations. You got this I promise.

MACK GAME

dmit, some of you went to this chapter first! Before we get into it, let's set your cell phone up for success first. Like I said in the intro, The Player is organized. If you want to be a Player and you don't have at least a smartphone, come on man. Get it together and get one there are so many dating apps and what not, it's too easy now! Anyway, when you are putting girls' phone number get their picture of their face. That way when you got eight thousand 'Jessica's in your phone you know which one you are talking to. Or have her first and last name but always have a pic. How to pass an objection, just say you want a pic of her for your contacts. If she objects still whatever, have a nick name, something so you

know who it is. Some of you are so into whatever you are into, that's all you can talk about. A Player is always current and is always on top of trends. Apps you should have is one that has news, sports and pop culture. Still be into what you are into, I got it, I love sports, but I know who Kylie Jenner is, I'm just saying. E!, CNN, Fox News, (gotta know both sides) ESPN app for an example is a good start to have. The reason is so you have something to talk about.

Dating apps/Social Media

For those with dating apps or on Social Media, three essential pics you should have. Your profile pic should be with you smiling (don't have to grit your teeth) a pic of you in the driver's seat of a car (if you have a car) and a full body pic. If you don't have a car, third pic can be whatever just don't look a moron and I know some of y'all like "but it could be a silly pic that would have her talk to me and ask me about it" That's weak sauce and you are going to learn what to say so that your words will lead to action you know? If you got

abs, show it off, let her know you packing the goods. Also, it'll weed out the wack girls who are like "I don't care about pics like that". Which is a lie, it's part of the reason why they sent you a message because you look good. So, we got three pic essentials, now how to describe yourself. Four things girls want to know from jump, if you got your own place, a car, job and kids. That all should be included within the first few sentences, that way you got all of that out of the way and it's not a surprise and she doesn't ask you those questions. You just want to get into flirt mode. If you don't have any or some of those things the only then just talk about you and what you are all about obviously but if you go to Harry Potter conventions every year don't mention that. Your profile should be something where any girl who reads it won't be like "He's a weirdo" That's the only goal. Some apps have drop downs, if you are one of those guys who doesn't want to mess with kids who have kids, and you are over twenty-one and looking for a girl over twenty-one and older, good luck. Take the L (Loss) and put the drop down "Kids ok" or whatever.

How to flirt with a girl online.

Some of you guys are like "about time". Think about this, you aren't the only guy getting at this girl. Saying 'Hey' or even "Hey Beautiful' isn't good enough. What I say is "Hey Beautiful on Beautiful". It might sound stupid, but the smart girls get it. It's unique and you can say 'Gorgeous on Gorgeous' whatever is going to make you stand out. It's about not calling them just 'beautiful' like all the hundreds of other messages. Even on apps where you can only message if you match, I still say that. It's all about keeping the routine and going with what works. If a girl says, "What does that mean?" just say "calling you simply 'beautiful' is an understatement". Then follow up with a simple "How are you?" This is where you go to work. When it comes to flirting, you must treat it like tennis, you want to go back and forth, no breaks or pauses in the conversations. That's why I say stay up on current events so you have something to talk about and learn everything you can about her. Everyone is asking for nudes, sending dick pics, not you. The goal at the end of the day is to

stand out, because your competition is trying to fuck her just like you. If she has kids, ask how old they are, what are their names. It's not creepy, it's showing interest in her life. Ask what her favorite color is, what her favorite flower is, what's her dream vacation spot, you ask questions that make her talk about her. If she asks why you are asking all these questions, just say you want to get to know her and call her out, ask what she wants to know about you. If you she starts talking about sex, ask what her fave positions are and what she likes and only tell her what you like if she asks. Like I said, it's back and forth like tennis. Don't force her into certain subjects, go with the flow and guide her to talking about sex. Like if she starts sending nudes or talks about sexual experiences with an ex or whoever, then that will set up to find out what she's into sexually. Even if she might send nudes, she still might not be into talking about sex. Let her start it off first so you don't sound like a desperate loser. Then find out what you need to know in order to fuck. You got to make it sound you are all about pleasing her. Do that, better chance she'll want

to fuck. DON'T SEND DICK PICS UNLESS SHE ASKS! You are different and smooth with it. Believe, me she will ask if she really wants to know. Especially when you show off the six pack and you show off part of your pelvis. She'll ask if you can go lower, then send it.

If she only has a pic of her face and not her body and you are curious of what her body looks like, just ask "you got any full body pics?" If she asks why, just say "I'm curious if your body is a beautiful as your face". That usually works with a little objection and if she does, move on ask a question to get her mind off the pic thing. If she's showing off her assets, and you want to see more, ask "any topless pics and pics from the back in a thong or less?" It's direct and she's not sending a whole bunch of pics trying to guess what you want to see. If she says she's not that type of girl, look, they all have them type of pics. Eventually, she will send them but the end of the day, the goal is to fuck her anyway so don't be that concerned if she doesn't send nudes right away. Just divert, say my bad, ask more questions, trying to get to know her. This

is crucial, cause if she's allergic to shellfish, you aren't going to take her to seafood restaurant on a date, right? Then you are on your phone trying to Google non seafood restaurants, embarrassing.

How to flirt with a girl you know

If you know the girl, casually through work, or you she's the one at the coffee shop you say 'hi' to or you've known her since Kindergarten, you always risk this blowing up in your face. Especially if you are nothing more than 'a friend'. How to break out of that is getting aggressive in talking. Saying 'I want to fuck' without saying 'I want to fuck'. How you do this is keep throwing in randomly how beautiful and sexy she is in random conversations. If she still doesn't get it, you play 'I've always had a crush on you' card and see where that goes. I'm not saying it always works but it's a start. That's why you had the 'make over'. You must look good, clothes sharp, car always clean, no bags of fast food in the back, your house or apartment immaculate. You must present the best package

as possible, because this girl you know is the hardest to fuck, because she knows a lot about you and never saw you that way. If she rejected you before, you got to hit with a new approach. Notice when she gets new boots. Let her know they look amazing on her If she colored her hair, or got a perm, let her know you love her hair. Even if you hate it, who cares. You're trying to fuck. Always interject a comment with how beautiful she is. Like if she shows you a picture of a sunset for an example, and if she says it's a beautiful pic, but not as beautiful as you. If you see her in a sexy outfit, put it out there that she looks sexy. Like I said, you must switch it up and throw her off guard. Make her look at you in a different way. If she complains about a bad date, ask her what her perfect date will be like and if its attainable, make it happen. If she wants to see a certain band, get tickets and invite her. If she says she's sick, say that you wish you could cater to her. If she asks how you are doing say, always amazing when I hear from you. I know some of y'all think this is corny and what not, I'm telling it works. If she says she had a long day and can't wait

to relax, tell her that you wish you could massage that smooth skin of hers. This is where you play tennis, Player!

You are looking for a reaction, what's her next move. She might say, that would be nice. If so, tell her know that you aren't giving her lip service. Let her know that you two would be hot together and you would love to get crazy deep inside her. Tell her what body part you like the most and that you always imagined what she would look like naked. See if she will send pics. Take a fucking chance. If you don't want to mess up the friendship I understand. Sometime there are risks not worth taking.

Now, when it comes to a co-worker. This is always tricky. You must work with this person, and you don't want to get accused of sexual harassment. If she asks for your number (which has happened to me) she wants to fuck most likely. It's your job not to fuck it up. Get the pussy and handle your business. You got your place set up for success, Do the damn thing. This is where you must play the ultimate tennis match. If she seems like she doesn't like you that way, move on. Don't

mess your paper up for pussy. Never worth it. The number one thing you have to find out when you try to fuck a coworker, is she crazy, does she get attached easily, will she try to get you in trouble because she wants to date now and you just wanted to smash and dash, be adults about it. Is she a "pop up girl", the type that will pop up at your place unannounced? You are a Player, you are on a schedule, you got other bitches to fuck, not just her. If she seems like she's any of those things, I don't care how hot she is, don't fuck her. No pussy is worth that headache. To find all that out, talk to her about her ex's. See to see how she was in previous relationships. Don't talk about sex with her unless she brings it up first. If your ex was boring or you were boring for her, just say we weren't "compatible being intimate". Tennis anyone? If she asks for details, ask her if she is sure and that you don't want to offend her. If she says you won't, then tell her. Once you've been talking for a while and you get the vibe that she might be down to fuck, ask her if she wants to hangout sometime. If she says no, move on. On to the next one.

QUICK HITS

What to expect from a girl in a certain age range.

18-23: Likes to party and go to club and bar. Very into what's happening and what's new, very versed on social media and what's trending. Especially with technology. Better be prepared to stay up all night Thursday-Saturday. Might be a mom, so college grads be prepared.

24-29: Might getting over her party stage but still likes to go out occasionally. Probably has baby daddy and trust issues. Going to have to work around that schedule of kids and work. Been around the block, heard most of the bullshit

before so you are gonna put in a little work to fuck and might be looking for a relationship.

30-36: Sort of the same for 24-30 but one or more baby daddies and possibly divorced.

Kids might be in the teens so you gotta deal with their bullshit and drama if you go to her place. They think all you are doing is trying to fuck their mom. Might have to win them over first. Expects you to be mature and have a job or car at least. Might like to go one occasionally to get away from their kid(s) so she might want to go to the bar or club. Heard a lot of the bullshit before, going to have to put it more work and might be looking for a relationship. Expects you to be experienced in bed so you gotta do the damn thing, Player!

37-45: Kids late teens or out of the house. If she has kids in the house, still baby daddy drama, so she won't have time your bullshit. You are must prove you got it together and not a little boy. That you are a real man on your grind, handling your business. Might give up the pussy easy or make you

work for it. It's a crap shoot. Heard all of the bullshit before. Possibly likes to go out for a drink or two and have a good time. Might want to bring her female friends along, so you will have to get their approval. Don't flirt with them, act like they aren't hot, even if they are (I know it sucks). If her friends come off shady and you think they would fuck, play tennis with them to make sure they aren't trying to test you for their girl, but only after you fuck first, then go after them. Remember the rules! Don't get caught, don't fuck up your pussy and bitches always front!

46 and beyond: You notice a trend, lol... sort of like the 37-45. Believe it or not, this is my favorite type of girl to mess with, been around the block, gonna keep it real with you either looking to settle down or just wants to fuck. Kids more than likely out of the house or very close to being out. Little or no baby daddy drama. Might have some disposable income, so could be a potential sugar mama situation, so enjoy the ride, Player!

What to expect from a girl from a certain region:

East/MidWest: Only major difference is how they see themselves politically, East more liberal and Midwest more conservative so stay away from politics. Both type girls are passionate about their teams and like to go out to the bars and have a good time. East Coast girls, a little more fashionable and artsy than Midwest girls but not by much. Love their region very much.

South: More conservative, can drink a lot, so get it twisted. Not all like just Country Music, some only like Rap or Rock. Likes to be out in nature so expect to meet her friends and family in outdoor events. Can sniff out a Yankee (North East person) from a mile away. Handle your liquor and love football and you should be fine.

West: More liberal and more chill. Fashionista for the most part. Wants you to have it together and be about something

and be passionate about a cause. Lots of sport teams in the areas but doesn't talk about it that much. More concerned about what's going on the world. Always up on current events. (remember I told you get them news apps, this why).

OUTRO

That's it, if you don't want to read beyond this sentence then Happy Hunting. Do note only two things guaranteed, death and taxes. Even Michael Jordan didn't make every game winner. I'm not promising that with this you will fuck every bitch you encounter. This is just help those who don't know where to begin at all. I didn't want to write a long ass book because you don't have time for that. I don't either. I was talking to bitches while I was writing this book (don't fuck up your pussy, remember) literally. Hopefully this will be the corner stone to your success. What I wrote is what works for me and I hope it works for you. If you must tweak it so it works for you then do it. I'm not saying these

words are from God and if you don't use it you will fail. If the shoe fits wear it, if not kick it off as I once heard. I used to be like y'all, not really knowing what to say to girls. A lot of trial and error, mostly error. Now not really any errors. I'm not saying I'm perfect and this will make you perfect. That will be a damn lie and any guy telling you they smash every girl they talk to that's a lie too. It's all good now, because, Player, you got the tools for success. It's just your job to figure out which tool will help you for success. You got a great blueprint, this book will guide you to success and you'll be dripping in pussy and making her drip as well. Go get em, Player!

Printed in the United States
By Bookmasters